Jen's Place

Paint our Walls with Photos

JENNIFER ANICETO

AuthorHouse™
1663 Liberty Drive
Bloomington, IN 47403
www.authorhouse.com
Phone: 833-262-8899

Because of the dynamic nature of the Internet, any web addresses or links contained in this book may have changed since publication and may no longer be valid. The views expressed in this work are solely those of the author and do not necessarily reflect the views of the publisher, and the publisher hereby disclaims any responsibility for them.

This book is printed on acid-free paper.

ISBN: 978-1-6655-7336-8 (sc)
ISBN: 978-1-6655-7335-1 (e)

Library of Congress Control Number: 2022919059

Print information available on the last page.

Published by AuthorHouse 10/18/2022

authorHOUSE®

Jen's Place

Paint our Walls with Photos

PREFACE

2022... Post-pandemic times. Encouraged and inspired by a colleague to join, enticed by lucrative prices as giveaways to winners. Time slipped so fast not minding the hour of the day, doing my laundry. As I finished the laundry I decided to compose something to post since I still had the time to beat the deadline. 10 minutes and it was finished. Not much editing as I became used to writing by then, as I wrote articles for readcash. Fortunately, I won 2nd prize and that started it all. Now I became an addict. Addicted to posting articles every day and I started joining.

I join and looking back... I am very grateful for the push and enjoying my time joining the events. Now I have a collection of items from the prizes I have garnered in the events especially the t-shirts, - I am definitely a fan.

June 2022, I got sick and eventually my eldest had to walk me to work every day. And for those times, I told him to take pictures of the moon because the moon was shining so good and the view was ecstatic. He started taking pictures then, but prior that, he was already taking pictures and sent it to my messenger. Then I used those pictures as an inspiration in writing articles, made poems out of it. And that made me happy! Silently wishing, swept by amazement of the photos he produced. And to that, I decided to make "an exhibit at home" which requires a lot of hard work because I have to skim coat the walls to make the exhibit presentable. Although a temporary abode, but I'd like to make it special to us.

Painting our walls with his photos while the young one, Evan, with his laughter that echoes through our walls all day long. And now, writing and publishing a book with his photos – a memoir in the making.

EJ graduated elementary not with flying colors but I was most happy as he fulfilled his promise to graduate school. A rebel of his own but he took care of me while I was sick, "a heart needed repairing" he said. Writing this towards the end of August 2022, I was waiting for the results of the contest on "Mobile Photography", an event I joined to make an inclusion of the entry I submitted. It is a marvelous inclusion.

I, me and myself, is all there we have. Unfortunately, left with kids whom I fell in love with. And for a decade, nothing proves to be the best part of my life but having children. As they grow each day, each year... seeing them grow under my roof is an experience I would like to enrich. The more they grow, I more I long to see them through rough times in growing old. But they have proven resilient than I, because they taught me more than I could teach them. Living a life, able to experience to be in-love every day. As you look forward to go home into the arms of these little men, cuddling them, feeding them, telling them bed time stories – the bible story book with a request to start with "Once upon a time"... Oh! The memories linger, with all-time favorite story, Jona swallowed by the fish... hahaha! Boys! They love adventure even at such young age!

Worked in a self-publishing company for 10 years and this is my 1st book. I am excited! The making of my 1st book project. A realization of the plans we made to self-publish – Louella and I, a dear friend who lost her battle in fighting cervical cancer on the 6th of February, 2022. In the mist of dawn, about 3am, she knocked our door bidding me goodbye! She suggested to have a marathon publishing, publishing images. Never did I thought that this would be it.

Moments captured by a click!

I would have never thought that such beauty will be captured in a click!

Often times I click the camera, trying hard to capture the very beautiful moment right in front of me... Trying to freeze time as one slips into another moment after one has gone! And almost every time I failed. Disheartened I could only imagine the picturesque remains in my mind, forever more frozen as I opted to share them.

Time slips as swiftly as the wind blow. That moment is gone almost in an instant... knowingly how the moments were uncaptured is such a tormenting agony and a disappointment as those moments will no longer be repeated but will be long gone as the memory allows. Oh! How nice will it be able to share those moments where laughter and tears collide in a moment our minds can recall.

Then my son showed me images that he randomly caught! Moments he captured on the wee hours of dawn at our roof deck!

Oh! How lovely it was! Immerse in such a moment where the clouds are kissing the sun, as the sun rises! Seeing how the clouds dances with the winds in the early hours of the morning… ah! Wonderful, tantalizing to the sense, and even awakens the sleeping thoughts and be enticed to celebrate the moment as captured.

On the other hand, as the celebration ends… capturing another moment where the clouds are saying their goodbyes as darkness looms over the light… the evening is fast approaching! How repugnant it is to end but the sight still is unwavering!

Oh, the silhouette reflects the daunting moment as the light fades away! Feeding the imagination away where the creatures of the night are about to come out, as darkness abounds. And lo! Comes the bat... flying in the middle of the night in search of food. Whilst the spiders too are out, spinning their thread to capture the insects that loom somewhere hidden not afar!

Oh! How interesting the stories to be told on these wonderful moments captured with a click! Runs the imagination wild into the fantasies we all sought to create as the moments pass away!

Samsung Triple Camera
Shot with my Eathan's A22

Come back to nature and enjoy it to its fullest, - Nature at its finest. A picturesque look at the beach, with the sunrise and sunset at every start and end of the day. A never-ending cycle that we all look forward each day. Altogether the ecosystem that surrounds it, a blessing that collides with man and its habitat, captivating to the searching soul to be filled with lingering joy over the chaos of city life! Rekindles the primal instinct that adjoins man and nature, forged a long time ago.

Mother Nature provides an endearing warmth, embracing every soul, bringing in peace and solitude. An unmatched subtleness that feeds and relaxes man's inner soul. Reinvigorates anyone that who seeks, healing his core allowing a rebuild. Breathe... slowly breathe and fill it up the air that cleanses.

Our provincial home is blest with a backyard beach, where fish fries abound together with the lush mangroves that surrounds it, creating a habitat suitable for an ecosystem. It's a government project that started years ago amidst the call for seaside rehabilitation, as the ecosystem has been greatly damaged, due to human settlement. Now, we are lucky to explore the horizon as it has created a good sandbar where many children are enjoying the sea without the fear of exploring far beyond.

In our local culture, it has been a practice to go and enjoy the beach during weekends especially when the climate has been unforgivingly hot. While others prefers the smoothness and ease of mountain exploration, especially when the budget is right, spending a weekend on mountain resorts. Also a lovely sight to behold.

Samsung Triple Camera
Shot with my Eathan's A22

Dancing with the sun as it brightens up the day and warms the cool breeze of dusk, telling us to rise as another day has unfold, in the early hours of morning sunshine. A lovely sight to behold, especially coming out from a cold night breeze, just befitting to start a buzzling day doing our chores. While others goes to work, up for a long day up ahead.

Wrapping it up with a beautiful sunset by the beach. A serene night I should say, creating a drowsy feel for a good night sleep. A picturesque scene by the sea, so to speak that not everyone has the luxury to enjoy! Oh! How heavenly! A perfect scene that chases the stress away! Letting the stress flow away into the depths of the sea... a soothing way of ending a day that only a few, enjoys. Thank God, we are a few who did!

15

Not every day we enjoy a beautiful sunrise or a sunset! So we might as well seat, relax and enjoy while it lasts...

As we talk about sunrise and sunsets... Ahhh! Let's explore the provincial heights and its scenery! Oh! Great is the walk with Mother Nature. The feel in the air & the soil, unceasingly amazing. The feel of the soil underneath your feet, the feel the bark of the tree on your hand, the feel of the air passing through your skin, wind blowing your hair up, tangling it more casting a spell that'll send you to fantasy land. So mesmerizingly awesome that'll send you to dreamland in a few, with the grass field as your bed, the outgrown root of the tree your pillow, the chirping birds as your lullaby... A rare luxury, the feel of the sun tangled with the cold breeze of the air touching your face as you behold a breath-taking sight of the sun rising from the horizon. The mixed feel of heat and coldness, hmmm, refreshing. The heat and exposure fills in the skin with the nutrients it needs, producing sweat that secretes the excessiveness of water evaporating into the mist. Reinvigorates the body, relieved from the piled up soreness inside, healing to the core. The spirit lifted up as something inside wallowing up was released. Released into the air, forever forgotten with the mist. hmmm, a good relief...

As we explore nature, we come to enjoy the scenery within our gasp! The trees dancing as the wind blows, the chirping birds singing out loud, serenading like a lover... Oh! The butterflies showcasing their colors as they visit each flower that blooms. While the bees and bugs too, show off a little competition with their colors and buzzling sounds. Interactive as ever as the ecosystem lives. While the interplay continues, as dusk comes along... While all other retires back to their nest to nurture themselves and enjoy the rest of the night sleeping, another play begins...

Another story to tell... as the dusk goes deeper, the creatures of the night slowly creeps. The spiders threading, ready to make traps for their preys, trapped in their silks and be wrapped into a cocoon to be preserved as food. Which is why men haunts spiders at night for their gaming battles..

The dogs too, howls at the slightest step detected that almost sound like a wolf scaring people away especially under the brightness of a full moon.

In the suburbs, it's most scary especially when an owl is present and electricity is just poor, a not well-lighted place. The hounds just unceasingly howls and the owl coockoo, like a real-scary creature that passes by. To a child it is a scary movie, clutch itself to whoever is present, seeking protection from a scare. When it's just a bunch of dogs rallying somewhere trying to meet its pack, mating perhaps.

The city. Less scary as people abounds and creeps in the night trying to have fun until dawn. Not minding that their body needs rest. But, let's set aside the city lights but there are some quite few catchy sceneries too. For nature is truly captivating despite.

Still scary for any child to go out at night, knowing that shadows abounds. Dark places exist when the lights are off or when power surge just happened and electricity hasn't been restored. Especially on stormy nights. When rain rules the night, the cool breeze is just as relaxing and frightening too. As the gust of the wind might become terrifying as it grows strong, while rain just lasts the whole night. Afraid that flood with strike anytime at night or any land slide that is about to happen, where darkness abounds, who wouldn't be scared?

Remembering the scary haunted houses we passed by when we were young. The stories they told that even in the scourging heat of mid sun, you can feel the chill in the air. The eerie feeling that runs through your veins up to your neckline while the goosebumps never ceases, scares any kid that passes by at noon... Oh! Those moments really never fail to captivate a kid's wild imagination, come rushing and running far away from the house as much as possible. Never to pass by there again, especially alone. Others, pack up with their faith and prayed the "Hail Mary's" and "Our Father" over and over again, just to overcome the fear! Such days...

More on when it rains, the mud that is stuck at your feet. The slippery road that caused you to stumble as you wildly run towards safe heaven is just too much sometimes. As scary as it was, the laughs after the scare is just too genuine to ever care about embarrassment. Remembering those days, good old days, were just as good as it was just yesterday.

However... I find it nice to feel the cleansing effect of every rain that pours. Each time, helps you breathe clean air, devoid of dusts that abounds the air. Refreshing winds that blow, relaxing. And the next night, the frog singing out loud happily as the water swarms. Hmmm, befittingly for them while us, suffers walking through mud and mud holes that could be slippery to walk on.

Ahh! Rain. Someone posted a picture, a photo of his bike drenched in the rain. I love the drama it presents. A lone wolf, traveled so far, trying to find his destination but by far unreachable. Loving the idea that the rain cleanses that desire every time and finds his resolute to continue his pace until he has arrived. The cleansing it does, making the desire and destination pure as ever!

Yes... The rain has that effect on me. Cleanses the sorrow and sadness away... Leaving a refreshed feeling every time. Like an old scar, little by little it disappears in the passage of time. Or leaving the obvious physical scar but heals in time, when you allowed yourself to cleanse it.

Oh! How I loved it when it rains, but I don't like to be wet! What an irony! Lolz.

In other countries, seasons change while here, summer and rainfall are interchangeable these days. Perhaps suffering from EL Nido and EL Nino.

While season changes, occasions as well. Another year that went by and the kids are all grown up. Unexpectedly the bond between brothers is tight. It was such a heart-warming experience knowing kuya bought cake for bunso on his birthday, out from his own pocket. While he earns some money out of trade he made 2 days before his brother's birthday. Oh! How wonderful and I am proud of how kuya has turned out to be as he grows older by the year! Looking out for his brother. And most importantly, he knows his money. How his spending ways have matured! And I am just so glad, it paid so well.

Thinking about it while I sit on my seat typing this, made me think that passing by this life will not be complicated for me... they may be young but they are ready. Yet, in kuya's young mind he is still not ready... hmmm... well, he is there! Perhaps, a little more time... Oh! Surely, but not yet... Not anywhere soon! We still have to paint our walls, more with his photos and bunso has to be circumcised first... and lots of huggies and cuddles to come!

Ah, recording this time as the toughest part of our family's history yet the sweetest! Making it all more valuable to fight, for this is that part of life that matters the most! Money, can and will be earned but the most beautiful part of life is how treasures of the heart has seen us through darkest moments in our lives! Never can be traded with the luxury that will fade in time. These beautiful moments that embrace us, enveloping the heart, igniting it to look towards the horizon for the sun will surely shine while the rains surely cleanses leaving out the remnants of the tragedy! Hahaha! Majestic isn't it? How these moments magically turns tragedy into a masterpiece! A work of art that enriches human experience, that reminiscing in time makes you proud of what we have become! Our family had become! Oh thank you so much oh Lord for making this happen.

As nature embraces changes of times... Man and nature embraces their fate. As man being part of nature, it has its own creation to appreciate what nature offers. As nature collides with man's creation. In the vastness of the sea, man has crossed miles to reach the new horizons. Discovering new lands to thrive on and continues to do so in the passage of time. Like the sea, the mountains, everly isolated, man explored it depths... into the depth of its world. Man turns nature as its source of its produce...

Making way for developments and building of cityscapes. Now becoming more alluring as ever.

Right, just so timely a car passes by and lo! Capturing a perfect scene, conveying when man collides with nature! So amazingly nice! A serene joy ride down the suburbs, moving away from the city buzz and lights, an alluring thought that nourishes the soul. Taking away all the worries and stresses of daily life. Away from the confusing noise... a refreshing green scenery that rekindles the cool, soothing touch that nature brings. Imminently radiating to the mind that instantly relaxes. Enjoying the moment, for a moment to pass by, only to linger as memory forevermore.

And still, man prefers to go back into the warm loving embrace. Into the secluded place where man's destructive ways haven't reached. Far beyond the grasp of one's imagination, where nature feels untouched. Where fairies, feels like, they still exists. The mysteries that dances into unknown abyss, deep into the forest. Far, far away where tinkerbell still exists and pixie dust unceasingly flows out from its source… a magical adventure when magical creatures exist… where you'll enjoy watching and appreciating beautifully colored creatures with its magical powers… as hobbits goes out in plowing the fields with their beautifully built houses. Darves and elves too co-exists it's like living in a fairy tale, with a lot of interesting stories to be told, centuries old! Bringing in light and excited children for bedtime stories… the innocence of their youth! Wouldn't it be lovely!

Off beyond compare, still the solace nature brings. The excitement on passing through troughs, streams, muddy lakes... indulging yourself a good swim on the lake, haunting for food. Undiscovered tracks that leads nowhere or ends in a cave. Ha! Such an adventure...

While at the end of the day we go back to our small house, exhausted. Where a refreshing bath soothe away the soreness the hurts every nerve of the body. Coming home to your loved ones where you share cries and laughter, ending the day with stories of today and cuddles you until you all fall asleep! We all do look forward for that ayt? Hmmm... Just as everyday life goes on... We enjoy life as we live.

Into the loving arms of our beloved, safe and secure. Another moment to cherish and another moment to share, leaving nothing but a lifetime of memories to treasure! Life is short and we never know when it ends... We might as well spend it, cherishing every moments that passes by. Passing down the memory lane whenever we have the opportunity. While I am presented with the rarest opportunity, I am taking advantage of it and share it with people with whom I hold dear.

While I will be given the opportunity to leave behind a legacy that only few enjoys, recording this moment is a pleasure to behold.

It's just a simple treasure. Nothing much for I cannot afford anything more than I can present. The memory I left behind for my sons and grandchildren to read. Passing on the love and care. Telling them that moment this was composed, all the love and happiness was poured into this. Imperfect as it is but the heartfelt warmth with remain forever in our hearts. Warming the soul at times of need. Helpless but strong.

In the loving memory of Louella Pace. Thank you geng for these opportunities, and the push to write, despite all doubts. You will always be part of my household and as short as it was, our journey together was for a lifetime. The things we claimed together and conquered. We will miss you, especially the kids for spoiling them with your bribes! You will remain in our hearts. Thank you for redefining friendship to its core! Never would I thought that it be this way! Yes, it was definitely a ride. As you suggested, the photo book is my 1st book, never did it occurred to me. As I laughed at your suggestion, I am witnessing and embracing the result – who would have thought a perfect opportunity to publish. –ahhhh, no editing ayt! Now I know how it means…

To my boys… EJ and Evan Anthony… Thank you, and mommy will always love you very much! Continue to love and care for each other and never forget our memories! Tell mommy your troubles and always trust mommy will maximize effort to understand always. She will one day fade away and here is a gift to always remember those times… When time is rough, there will always be but remember always you have each other. Our bond will never break but will only grow strong as the years will pass, -do continue to hold on to each other.

To my little sister! We have shared this journey together and I am glad we did. Take care of the little girl, the only rose amongst the thorns.

<u>To our eldest!</u> Hmmmm... Ours was a rough ride and despite all the pains we been through, we remain. Our endeavor pushed us through all these years that has been the foundation, the building blocks of the principles that we hold dear, preserver to protect. A different kind of bond that lasted beyond the realms we ever thought off. Misunderstandings we sought through and mended in time. We can only look forward for the fortunes in the near future, and now, publishing together books we never dreamed of pursuing. A vision that used to be with a friend now gone, and have you to share this journey with, is more than a privilege and honor, redefining the bond we had. Rekindling the fire that burn in our hearts, long before our generation ever existed. Thank you for sharing this journey with me.

<u>To Authorsolutions,</u> thank you for the homage! It has been a wonderful ride. And for this opportunity to publish, oh! So, so, so wonderful gift to share with us and for us to share with our FAMILY and FRIENDs. My utmost gratitude.

My colleagues, teammates and friends... It has been a wonderful experience. The memories will be remembered...

To my family... Thank you.

Especial thanks to _Glen Cañete_, together with his wife –**_Lourdes and family_**, my sincerest gratitude for the opportunity to explore writing for the 1st time in all these years. Marking this as a remarkable stepping stone towards the achievement of this goal to publish. Without him, nothing in this book is possible. For giving me the trust that even I do not trust myself that I am capable of writing my dreams and thoughts into a reality that I lived in. For trusting me, giving me the confidence to write when I don't have an audience to write for but myself! I wouldn't have gone this far without that ounce of belief and trust, and for this I am truly grateful all my life! My prayers for good health, success and bounty due for you and family! Thank you so much!

Printed in the United States
by Baker & Taylor Publisher Services